# Life Cycle of a
# Chicken

## Angela Royston

Heinemann Library
Chicago, Illinois

Designed by Celia Floyd
Illustrations by Alan Fraser
Printed in Hong Kong / China

03
10 9 8 7 6 5 4

The Library of Congress has cataloged the hardcover version of this book as follows:

**Library of Congress Cataloging-in-Publication Data**
Royston, Angela.
    Life cycle of a chicken / by Angela Royston.
        p.    cm.
    Includes bibliographical references and index.
    Summary: Introduces the mating, hatching, life cycle, eating,
predators, and lifespan of chickens.
    ISBN 1-57572-698-X (lib. bdg.)
    1. Chickens--Life cycles--Juvenile literature.  2. Leghorns
(Poultry)--Life cycles--Juvenile literature.  [1. Chickens.]
I. Title.
SF487.5.R694   1998
636.5--dc21                                          98-10754
                                                        CIP
                                                        AC

Paperback ISBN 1-57572-474-X

**Acknowledgments**
The Publisher would like to thank the following for permission to reproduce
photographs: Bruce Coleman/Jane Burton pp. 9, 12; Heather Angel p. 8;
NHPA/William Paton p. 24, NHPA/Manfred Danegger p. 25; Oxford Scientific
Films/David Thompson p. 11, Oxford Scientific Films/Michael Leach p. 13, Oxford
Scientific Films/G. I. Bernard pp. 26-27; Photo Researchers Inc./Tim Davis p. 10, Photo
Researchers Inc./Kenneth H. Thomas pp. 14, 23; Roger Scruton pp. 4, 5, 6, 7, 15, 16,
17, 18, 19, 20, 21, 22.

Cover photograph: Britstock-IFA/Bernd Ducke.

Our thanks to Dr. Bryan Howard, University of Sheffield, in the preparation
of this edition.

# Contents

# Meet the Chickens

Chickens are birds. They have feathers, wings, and a **beak**. Different kinds of chickens have different colored feathers.

Egg

3 weeks

1 day old

The chicken in this book is a White Leghorn **cockerel.** He began life inside an egg. The egg was laid by his mother, a White Leghorn hen.

7 weeks

1 year

# The Eggs are Laid

The mother hen laid the egg in a nest. Every day she lays another egg and now there are six eggs in the nest.

Egg

3 weeks

I day old

The mother hen sits on the eggs to keep them warm. Inside each egg a new chick is growing.

7 weeks

1 year

# Hatching 3 weeks later

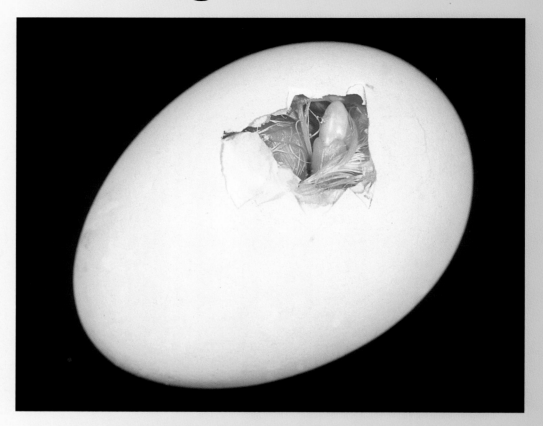

The eggs are beginning to **hatch**.
The chick uses its **beak** to chip a
hole in the shell.

8

Egg    3 weeks     I day old

The chick chips a hole all around
the egg. Now it uses its body to
push the egg apart. The little chick
is wet and tired.

7 weeks

1 year

10

Very soon its soft, **downy** feathers have dried. The little chick stands up and looks around.

Egg

3 weeks

I day old

This chick has just **hatched** too.
Soon all the chicks have left the
eggs and are cheeping loudly.

7 weeks

1 year

The little chicks drink water and eat seeds among the straw. They stay close together and follow the mother hen wherever she goes.

Egg     3 weeks     1 day old

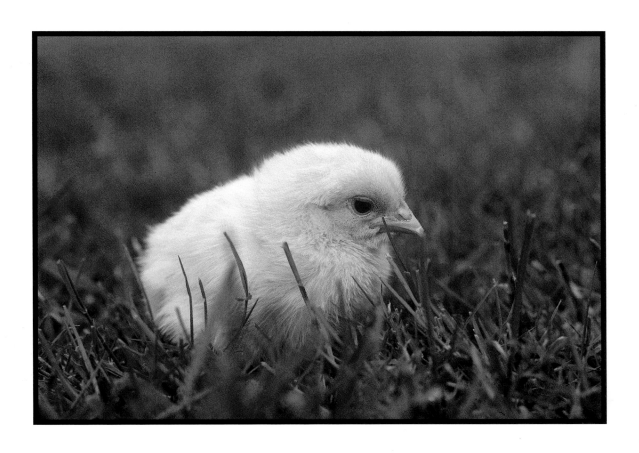

This chick has been separated from his mother. He listens for his mother clucking and runs after her.

7 weeks

1 year

# Young Chicken  7 weeks old

The chicks are bigger now, but they still shelter under their mother's wing. New, white feathers have grown in place of the yellow **down**.

Egg

3 weeks

I day old

The young **cockerel** has long tail feathers and a red **comb** on top of his head.

7 weeks

I year

# 2 months

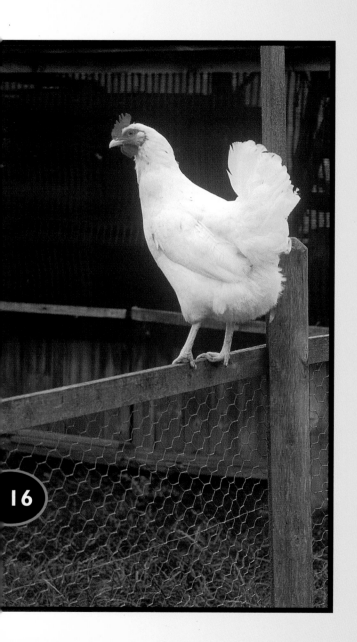

The chickens leave their mother and live in the **chicken run** with the other hens. Here the **cockerel** has flown up onto the fence to have a look around.

Egg     3 weeks     I day old

Now he pecks among the grass looking for seeds and worms to eat. He swallows his food whole and it is ground up in a stomach called a **gizzard**.

7 weeks

1 year

# Laying Eggs 5 months

The chickens are nearly full grown. This hen sits in one of the egg boxes in the hen house. She clucks loudly and then climbs out.

Egg

3 weeks

1 day old

She has just laid her first egg! From now on she will lay an egg almost every day. Her eggs have not been **fertilized**, so there are no chicks growing inside them.

7 weeks

1 year

The young **cockerel** struts around the farmyard. He watches carefully over several young hens. If one wanders off, he chases it back.

| Egg | 3 weeks | I day old |

The cockerel protects these hens from danger. If another cockerel comes near one of them, he chases it away.

7 weeks

1 year

# Mating

This hen is ready to **mate**. The young **cockerel** mates with her and **fertilizes** her eggs. She lays the eggs and sits on them.

Egg

3 weeks

1 day old

The eggs have **hatched** and there is a new **brood** of chicks. The hen looks after them, but the cockerel keeps a close eye on them too.

7 weeks

1 year

# Danger!

Very early one morning a fox climbs into the **chicken run**. He is a predator. At first the chickens do not see him.

Egg          3 weeks          I day old

The fox grabs a hen. The **cockerel** and the other chickens squawk and flap, but the fox jumps out of the chicken run and hurries away.

7 weeks

1 year

# The Farmyard

The cockerel has a busy life. He watches over the hens and chicks and from time to time he crows loudly.

He will stay on the farm until he dies. He may live until he is about ten years old, if the fox doesn't catch him.

# Life Cycle

## Eggs

1

## Hatching

2

## Chick

3

# Young Chicken

**4**

**5**

# Cockerel

# Fact File

A hen lays between 100 and 300 eggs a year, but not more than one a day.

The shell forms around the egg inside the hen's body. It takes about a day for the egg to form before it is ready to be laid.

People have kept chickens for over 3,000 years. They collect their eggs and eat them.

Chickens are probably the most common bird in the world. There are more than 10 billion (10,000,000,000) of them.

# Glossary

**beak**  hard covering of a bird's mouth

**brood**  a group of birds that hatch at the same time

**chicken run**  an area of fenced-in ground near a hen house

**cockerel**  a young male chicken

**comb**  a fleshy red crest on the top of a chicken's head

**down**  soft feathers

**fertilizes**  a female egg is fertilized when it joins with a sperm from a male

**gizzard**  a special stomach for grinding up food before it passes into the chicken's second stomach

**hatch**  to be born out of an egg

**mate**  when a male and a female come together to produce babies

# More Books to Read

Back, Christine. *Chicken and Egg.* Parsippany, NJ: Silver Burdett Press. 1991.

Legg, Gerald & Salariya, David. *From Egg to Chicken.* Danbury, CT: Watts, Franklin Inc. 1998.

Stone, Lynn. *Chickens.* Vero Beach, FL: Rourke Corp. 1990.

# Index